**Editorial Project Manager**
Mara Ellen Guckian

**Editor-in-Chief**
Sharon Coan, M.S. Ed.

**Art Director**
CJae Froshay

**Cover Artist**
Brenda DiAntonis

**Art Manager**
Kevin Barnes

**Imaging**
Temo Parra

**Product Manager**
Phil Garcia

**Publisher**
Mary D. Smith, M.S. Ed.

# Money

Pre K–1

**Author**

*Jennifer Kern, M.A.*

*Teacher Created Resources, Inc.*
6421 Industry Way
Westminster, CA 92683
www.teachercreated.com

**ISBN: 978-0-7439-3388-9**

©2003 Teacher Created Resources, Inc.
Reprinted, 2012
Made in U.S.A.

S0-AKA-989

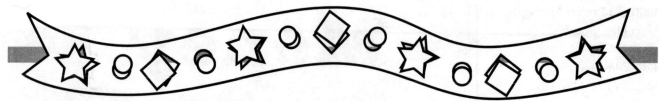

# Table of Contents

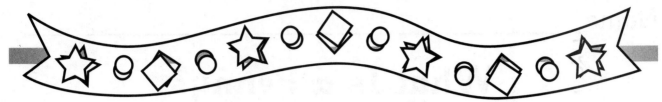

# Introduction

Getting children ready for academic success starts early. It is important, in these early years, to shape children's attitudes towards school and learning in a positive manner. The ultimate purpose of this series is to promote children's development and learning in an exciting manner. Young children need lots of repetition and directions that are simply worded. The activities need to be enjoyable and visually stimulating. This series was developed with those goals in mind. Each activity book is designed to introduce young learners to new concepts and to reinforce ones already learned. The pages are great for enrichment, classroom practice, tutoring, home schooling, or just for fun.

Money concepts are vital in the teaching of mathematics and are life skills that will be used again and again. Beginning in primary grades, students may use money to buy bubble gum or candy from a vending machine, buy soda from a vending machine, play a game at an arcade, or play a song in a juke box. Some children may choose to save their coins in a bank or jar. Whatever the choice, experiences with money start early and they continue throughout life. At the beginning stages, primary teachers focus on standards that include recognition of the penny, nickel, dime, and quarter, as well as each coin's value. Once these skills are mastered, students are ready to begin counting the value of different coins.

This book introduces students to basic concepts of money while incorporating other important mathematical standards such as patterning, graphing, counting, comparing sizes, and addition. Many of these activities can be reinforced with real coins as manipulatives by simply laying the real coins on top of the coins pictured to compare and count. Learning about money is fun because it is already a part of students' everyday lives. They will enjoy experimenting with the activities in this book and applying it whenever they can!

## National Standards for Money in Primary Grades

### Math as Problem Solving and Reasoning

- Students will apply money to virtual real-life situations such as buying small toys.
- Students will begin to understand the concept of money and its worth.

### Mathematical Connections

- Students will begin to understand how the knowledge of money concepts relate to real world situations.
- Students will apply other mathematical concepts such as comparing sizes, counting, adding, patterning, and graphing to pennies, nickels, dimes, and quarters.

### Number Sense and Numeration

- Students will begin to compute money values and add money.
- Students will count by ones, fives, and tens.

### Concepts of Whole Number Operations

- Students will solve problems requiring them to count money and add money.

### Patterns and Relationships

- Students will identify differences in pennies, nickels, dimes, and quarters. They will experiment with patterns and identify size differences in coins.

Name _____

# What Is a Penny?

This is a penny.   Each penny has a front and a back.

The front of the penny has a picture of Abraham Lincoln.  Lincoln was the 16th president of the United States.  Some people refer to the front of the coin as *heads*.

The back of the penny has a picture of the Lincoln Memorial which is located in Washington, D.C., U.S.A.  Some people refer to the back of the coin as *tails*.

A penny is worth one cent.  There are 100 pennies in a dollar.

The penny is the only coin that is made of copper and is brown.

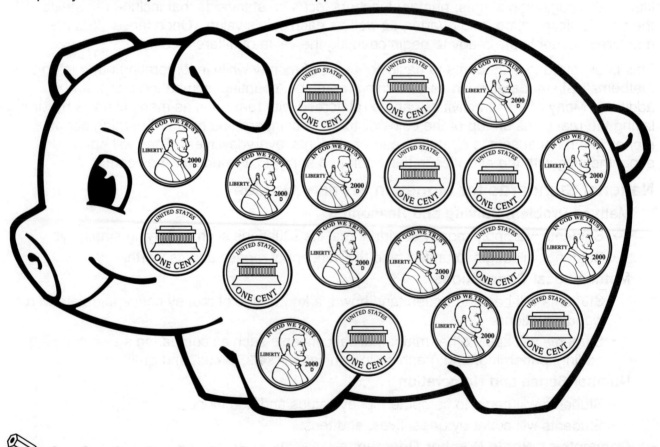

**Directions:**  Color each penny with the front side, or *heads* side, with a brown crayon.  Color each penny with the back side, or *tails* side, with a blue crayon.

Name _____

# Identifying Pennies

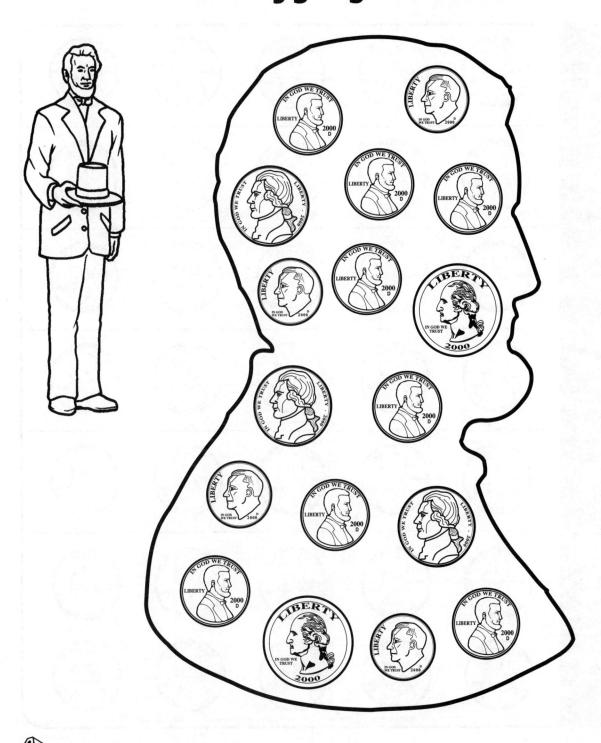

**Directions:** Color the coins that are pennies with a brown crayon. Put an **X** on each coin that is not a penny.

Name _____

# Counting Pennies

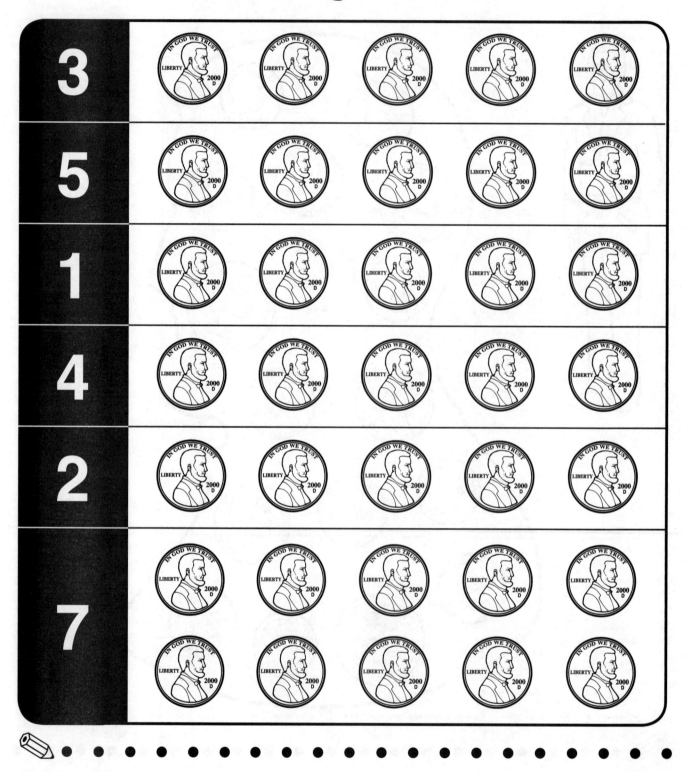

**Directions:** Look at the number at the beginning of each row of pennies. Color that number of pennies.

Name _____

# Buying with Pennies

A penny is worth one cent.  1 penny = 1¢

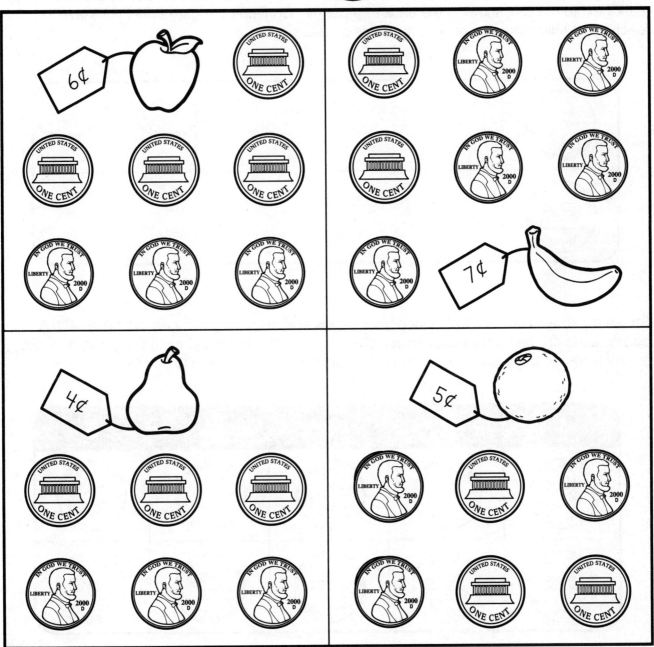

**Directions:** Look at the price tag on each item. Color the number of pennies needed to buy the item.

Name _____

# Tallying with Pennies

Shake a penny in your hands. Open your hands and drop the penny on the table. If the penny lands on the front side, or *heads* side, make a tally mark in the box next to the box showing the front of the penny. If the penny lands on the back side, or *tails* side, make a tally mark next to the box showing the back of a penny. Continue the game until you have reached 10 tally marks on either the *heads* or *tails* side.

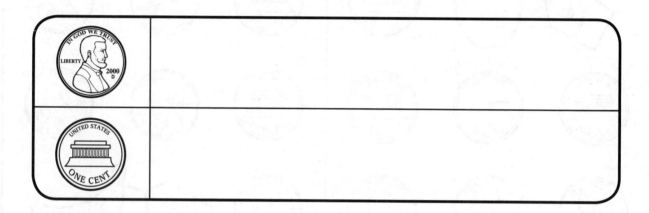

Shake a penny in your hands. Open your hands and drop the penny on the table. If the penny lands on the front side, or *heads* side, color in the *heads* penny in the column. If the penny lands on the back side, or *tails* side, color in the *tails* side. Do this five times.

| 1 | 2 | 3 | 4 | 5 |
|---|---|---|---|---|

**Directions:** Follow the directions above to use each type of tally table.

Name _____

# Patterning with Pennies

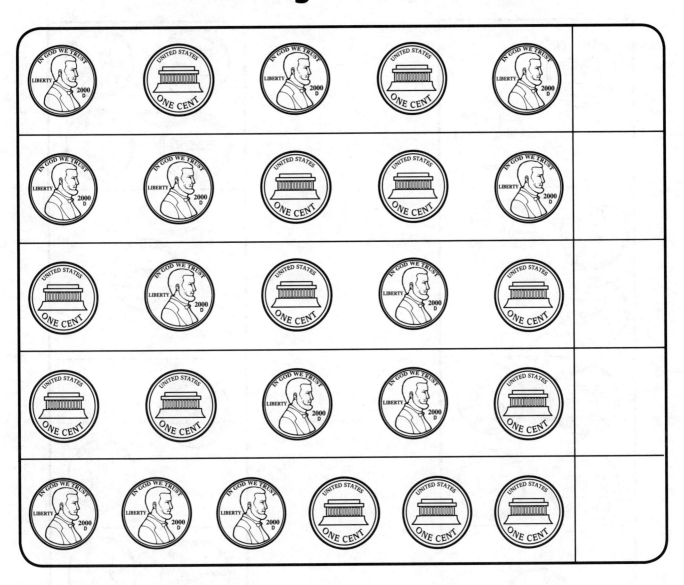

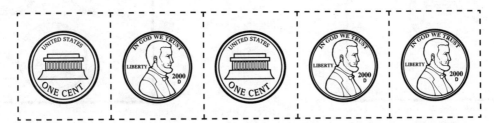

**Directions:** Look at the row of pennies. Determine whether the next penny in the pattern will be *heads* or *tails*. Cut out the correct pennies and paste them in the appropriate boxes.

# Matching Sets of Pennies

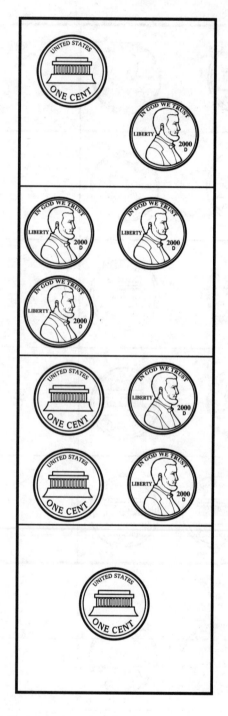

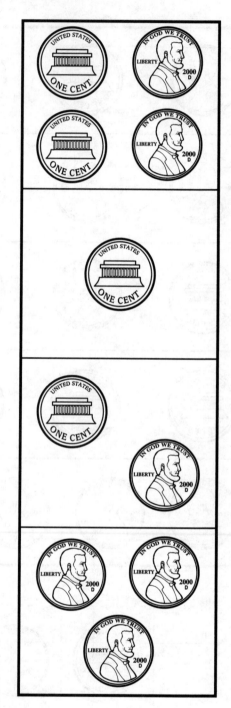

**Directions:** Look at the first box of pennies on the *left*. Find a box of pennies on the *right* that contains the same number of pennies. Draw a line to match the sets. Repeat with each of the other boxes of pennies.

Name_____

# Graphing Pennies

| Heads or Tails | | |
|:---:|:---:|:---:|
| **5** | | |
| **4** | | |
| **3** | | |
| **2** | | |
| **1** | | |

**Directions:** Count the pennies that show *heads*. Color that number of squares on the graph. Count the pennies that show *tails*. Color that number of squares on the graph.

Name _____

# What Is a Nickel?

 This is a nickel.    Each nickel has a front and a back.

The front of the nickel has a picture of President Thomas Jefferson. Jefferson was the third president of the United States. Some people refer to the front of the coin as *heads*.

The back of the nickel has a picture of Monticello which was his home. Some people refer to the back of the coin as *tails*.

A nickel is worth five cents. There are 20 nickels in a dollar.

**Directions:** Color each nickel with the front side, or *heads* side, with a green crayon. Color each nickel with the back side, or *tails* side, with an orange crayon.

# Name_____

# Identifying Nickels

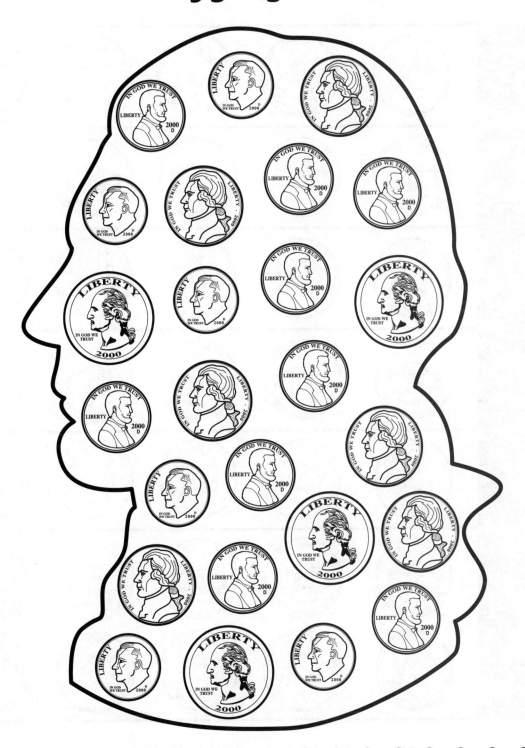

**Directions:** Color the coins that are nickels with a blue crayon. Put an **X** on each coin that is not a nickel.

# Counting Nickels

| | |
|---|---|
| **5** | |
| **3** | |
| **1** | |
| **2** | |
| **4** | |
| **8** | |

**Directions:** Look at the number at the front of each row of nickels. Color that number of nickels.

14

Name _____

# Buying with Nickels

A nickel is worth five cents.

1 nickel = 5¢

Count by fives to add nickels:    5        10        15        20        25

•••••••••••••••••••••

**Directions:** Look at the price tag on each item.  Color the number of nickels needed to buy the item.

Name _____

# Buying with Pennies and Nickels

**Directions:** Look at the price tag on each item. Color the number of pennies and nickels needed to buy the item.

Name _____

# Tallying with Nickels

Shake a nickel in your hands. Open your hands and drop the nickel on the table. If the nickel lands on the front side, or *heads* side, make a tally mark in the *heads* row. If the nickel lands on the back side, or *tails* side, make a tally mark in the *tails* row. Continue the game until you have reached 10 tally marks on either the *heads* or *tails* side.

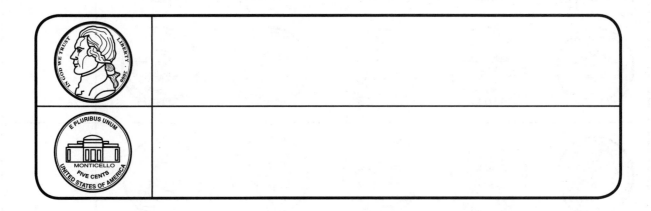

Shake a nickel in your hands. Open your hands and drop the nickel on the table. If the nickel lands on the front side, or *heads* side, color in the heads nickel in the column. If the nickel lands on the back side, color in the *tails* side. Do this five times.

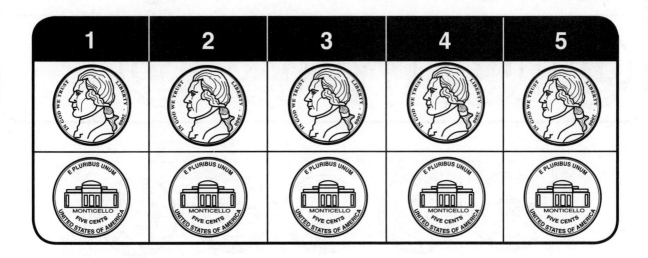

**Directions:** Follow the directions above to use each type of tally table.

Name _____

# Patterning with Nickels

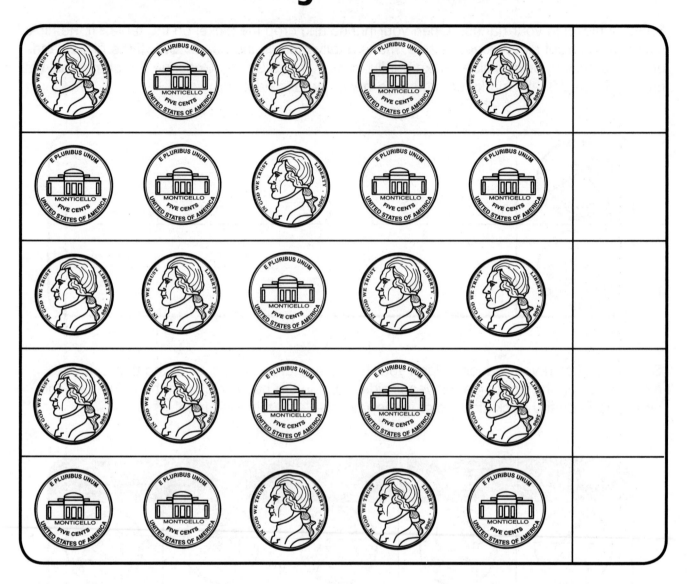

**Directions:** Look at the row of nickels. Determine whether the next nickel in the pattern will be *heads* or *tails*. Cut out the correct nickels and paste them in the appropriate boxes.

Name _____

# Patterning with Pennies
# and Nickels

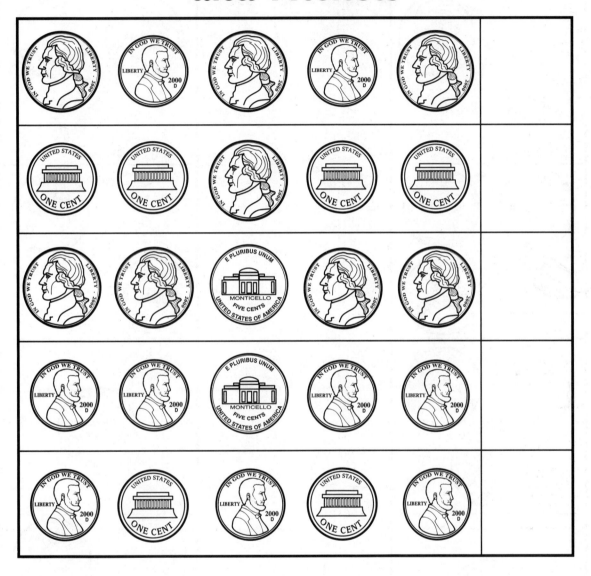

**Directions:** Look at the row of pennies and nickels. Determine whether the next coin in the pattern will be a penny or a nickel. Cut out the correct coins and paste them in the appropriate box.

# Name _____

# Matching Sets of Nickels

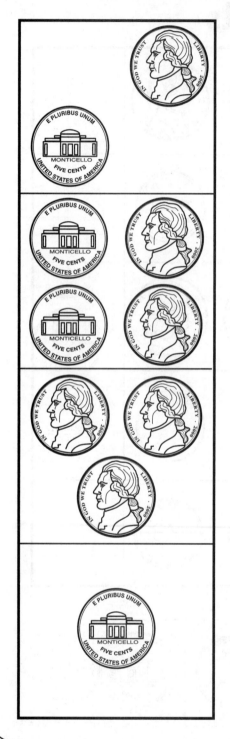

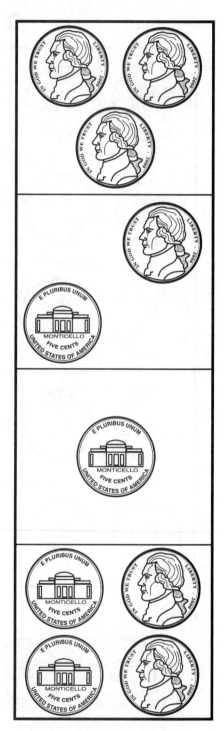

**Directions:** Look at the first box of nickels on the *left*. Find a box of nickels on the *right* that contains the same number of nickels. Draw a line to match the sets. Repeat with each of the other boxes of nickels.

# Matching Sets of Pennies and Nickels

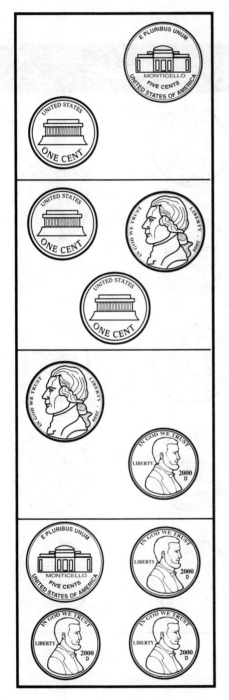

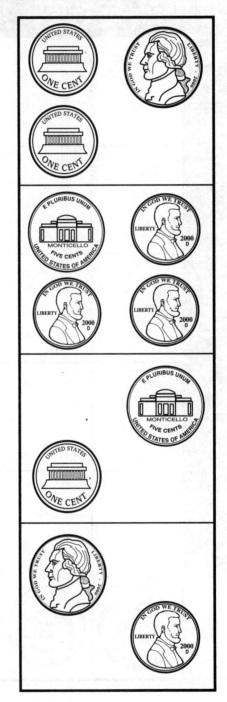

 ● ● ● ● ● ● ● ● ● ● ● ● ● ● ● ● ● ● ● ●

**Directions:** Look at the first box of pennies and nickels on the *left*. Find a box of pennies and nickels on the *right* that contains the same amount. Draw a line to match the set. Repeat with each of the other boxes of coins.

Name _____

# Graphing Nickels

| Heads or Tails | | |
|:---:|:---:|:---:|
| 5 | | |
| 4 | | |
| 3 | | |
| 2 | | |
| 1 | | |
| | (heads) | (tails) |

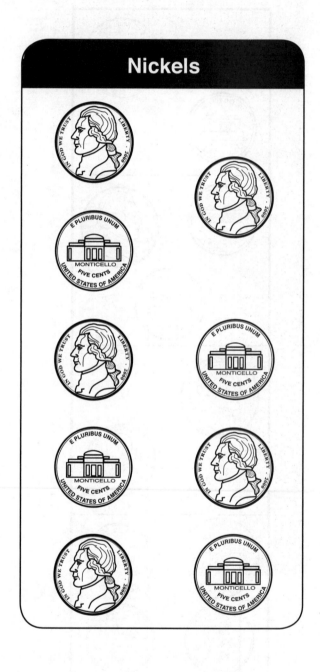

**Nickels**

**Directions:** Count the nickels that show *heads*. Color that number of squares on the graph. Count the nickels that show *tails*. Color that number of squares on the graph.

# Name _____

# Graphing Pennies and Nickels

| Pennies and Nickels | | |
|---|---|---|
| 5 | | |
| 4 | | |
| 3 | | |
| 2 | | |
| 1 | | |
| |  | |

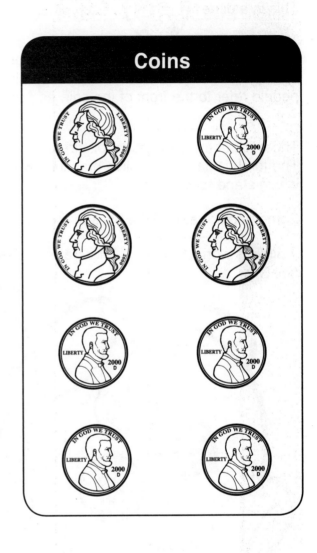

**Coins**

**Directions:** Count the pennies. Color that number of squares on the graph. Count the nickels. Color that number of squares on the graph.

Name _____

# What Is a Dime?

This is a dime.  Each dime has a front and a back.

The front of the dime has a picture of President Franklin D. Roosevelt on it. Franklin D. Roosevelt was the 32nd president of the United States. Some people refer to the front of the coin as *heads*.

The back of the dime has a picture of an upright torch, symbolizing freedom. The torch is flanked by olive branches which mean peace, and oak branches which stand for victory.

Some people refer to the back of the coin as *tails*.

A dime is worth 10 cents. There are 10 dimes in a dollar.

**Directions:** Color each dime with the front side, or *heads* side, with a red crayon. Color each dime with the back side, or *tails* side, with a blue crayon.

Name _____

# Identifying Dimes

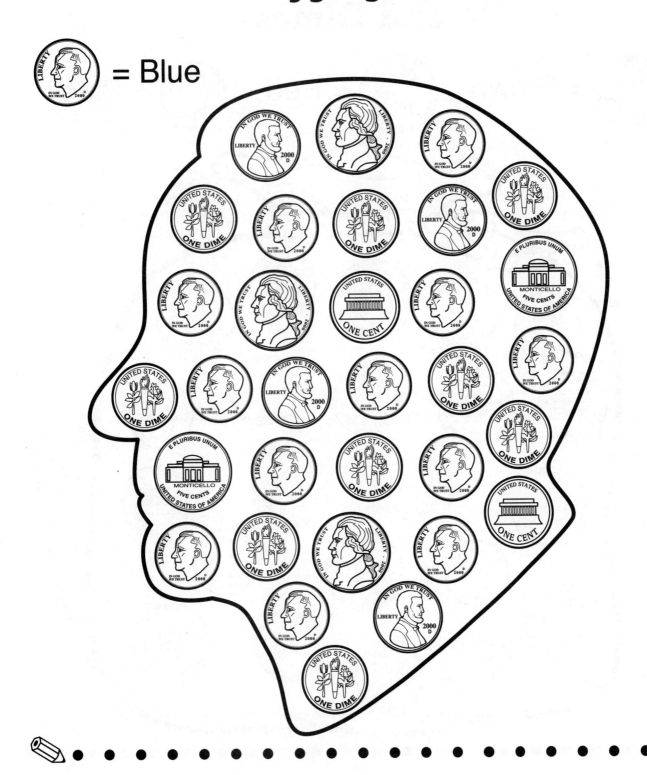

= Blue

**Directions:** Color the coins that are dimes with a blue crayon.  Put an **X** on each coin that is not a dime.

Name _____

# Identifying Pennies, Nickels, and Dimes

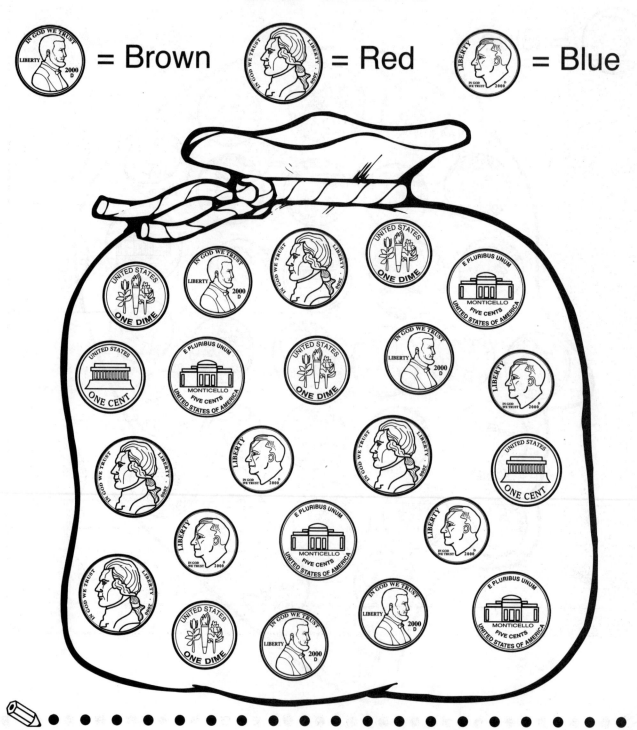

= Brown      = Red      = Blue

**Directions:** Color the pennies with a brown crayon. Color the nickels with a red crayon. Color the coins that are dimes with a blue crayon.

Name _____

# Counting Dimes

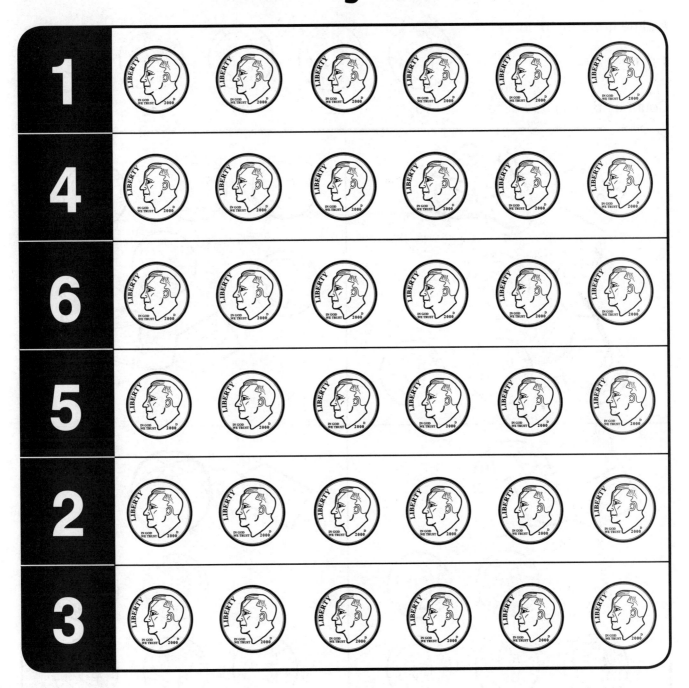

**Directions:** Look at the number at the beginning of each row of dimes. Color that number of dimes.

# Buying with Dimes

A dime is worth 10 cents.

1 dime = 10¢

Count by tens to add dimes:    10      20      30      40      50

 ● ● ● ● ● ● ● ● ● ● ● ● ● ● ● ● ● ● ● ● ● ● ● ● ●

**Directions:** Look at the price tag on each item. Color the number of dimes needed to buy the item.

# Buying with Pennies, Nickels, and Dimes

∎ • • • • • • • • • • • • • • • • • • • • • •

**Directions:** Look at the price tag on each item.  Color the number of pennies, nickels, and dimes needed to buy the item.

Name _____

# Tallying with Dimes

Shake a dime in your hands. Open your hands and drop the dime on the table. If the dime lands on the front side, or *heads* side, make a tally mark in the *heads* row. If the dime lands on the back side, or *tails* side, make a tally mark in the *tails* row. Continue the game until you have reached 10 tally marks on either the *heads* or *tails* side.

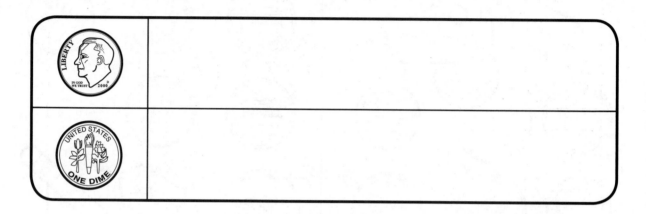

Shake a dime in your hands. Open your hands and drop the dime on the table. If the dime lands on the front side, or *heads* side, color in the *heads* dime in the column. If the dime lands on the back side, color in the *tails* side. Do this five times.

| 1 | 2 | 3 | 4 | 5 |
|---|---|---|---|---|
| | | | | |
| | | | | |

**Directions:** Follow the directions above to use each type of tally table.

Name _____

# Patterning with Dimes

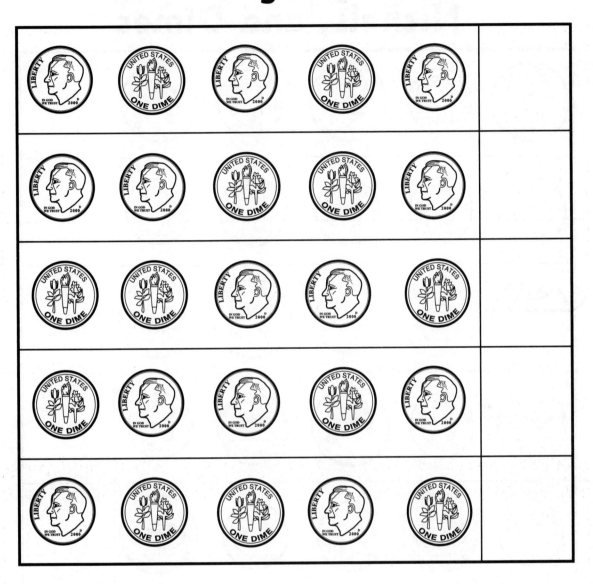

**Directions:** Look at the row of dimes. Determine whether the next dime in the pattern will be *heads* or *tails*. Cut out the correct dimes and paste them in the appropriate boxes.

Name _____

# Patterning with Pennies, Nickels, and Dimes

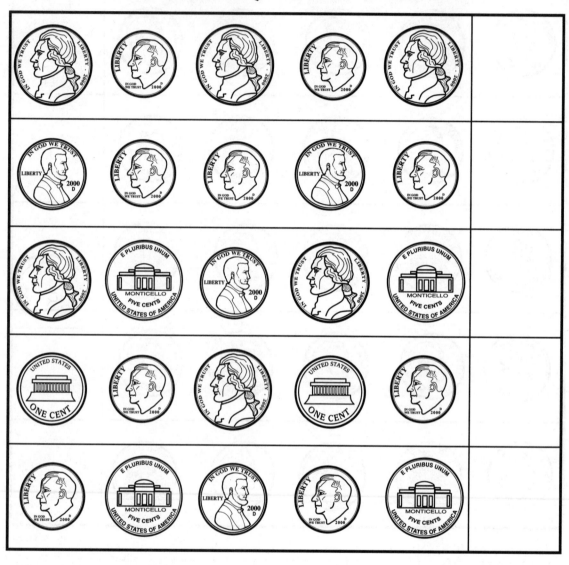

**Directions:** Look at the row of pennies, nickels, and dimes. Determine whether the next coin in the pattern will be a penny, a nickel, or a dime. Cut out the correct coins and paste them in the appropriate box.

Name _____

# Matching Sets of Dimes

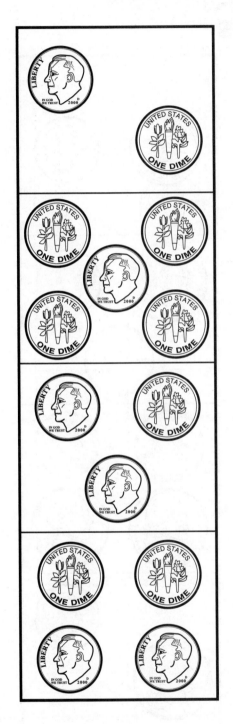

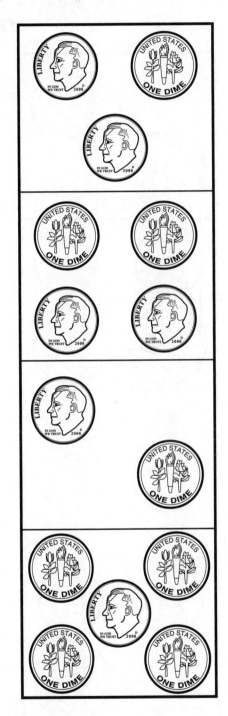

 ● ● ● ● ● ● ● ● ● ● ● ● ● ● ● ● ● ● ●

**Directions:** Look at the first box of dimes on the *left*. Find a box of dimes on the *right* that contains the same number of dimes. Draw a line to match the sets. Repeat with each of the other boxes of dimes.

Name _____

# Matching Sets of Pennies, Nickels, and Dimes

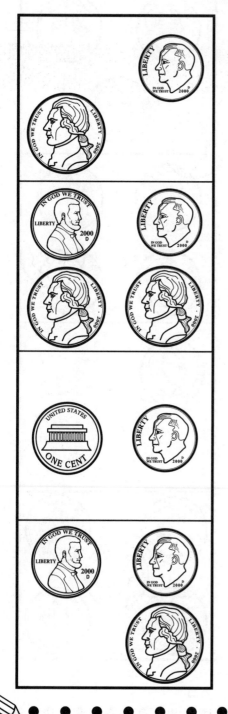

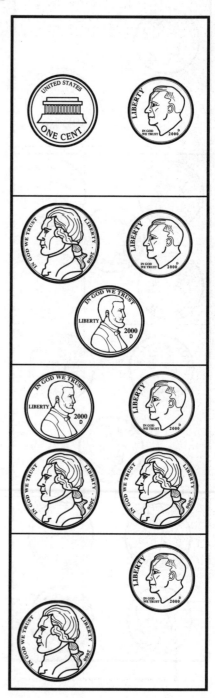

**Directions:** Look at the first box of pennies, nickels, and dimes on the *left*. Find a box of pennies, nickels, and dimes on the *right* that contains the same amount. Draw a line to match the set. Repeat with each of the other boxes of coins.

Name _____

# Graphing Dimes

| Heads or Tails | | |
|:---:|:---:|:---:|
| **5** | | |
| **4** | | |
| **3** | | |
| **2** | | |
| **1** | | |
| | Heads | Tails |

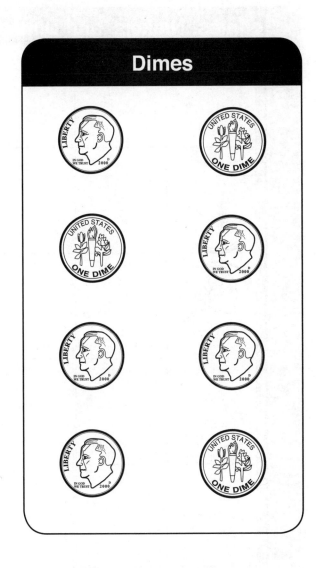

**Dimes**

**Directions:** Count the dimes that show *heads*.  Color that number of squares on the graph. Count the dimes that show *tails*.  Color that number of squares on the graph.

Name_____

# Graphing Pennies, Nickels, and Dimes

| Pennies, Nickels, and Dimes | | |
|---|---|---|
| 5 | | |
| 4 | | |
| 3 | | |
| 2 | | |
| 1 | | |

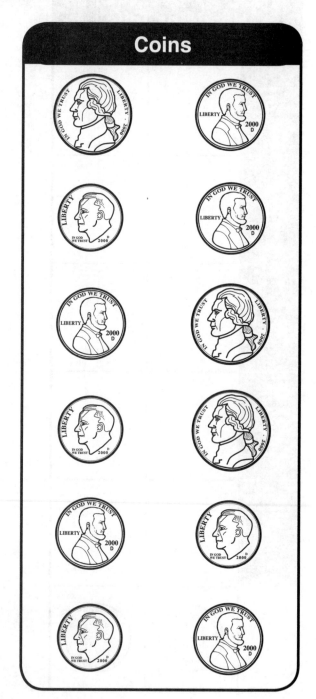

**Coins**

**Directions:** Count the pennies. Color that number of squares on the graph. Count the nickels. Color that number of squares on the graph. Count the dimes. Color that number of squares on the graph.

# Name _____

# What Is a Quarter?

This is a quarter.   Each quarter has a front and a back.

The front of the quarter has a picture of George Washington.  He was the first president of the United States.  Some people refer to the front of the coin as *heads*.

The back of the quarter has a picture of the bald eagle.  This symbolizes freedom.  Some people refer to the back of the coin as *tails*.

A quarter is worth 25 cents.  There are four quarters in a dollar.

**Directions:** Color each quarter with the front side, or *heads* side, with a red crayon.  Color each quarter with the back side, or *tails* side, with a blue crayon.

Name _____

# Identifying Quarters

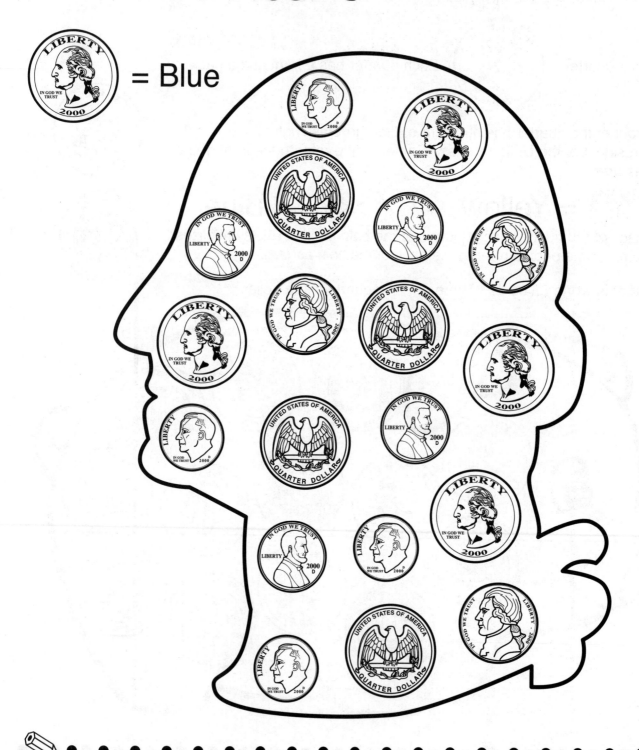

= Blue

**Directions:** Color the coins that are quarters with a blue crayon. Put an **X** on each coin that is not a quarter.

Name _____

# Identifying Pennies, Nickels, Dimes, and Quarters

 = Red           = Green

 = Yellow           = Blue

**Directions:** Color the pennies with a red crayon. Color the nickels with a yellow crayon. Color the dimes with a green crayon. Color the coins that are quarters with a blue crayon.

# Counting Quarters

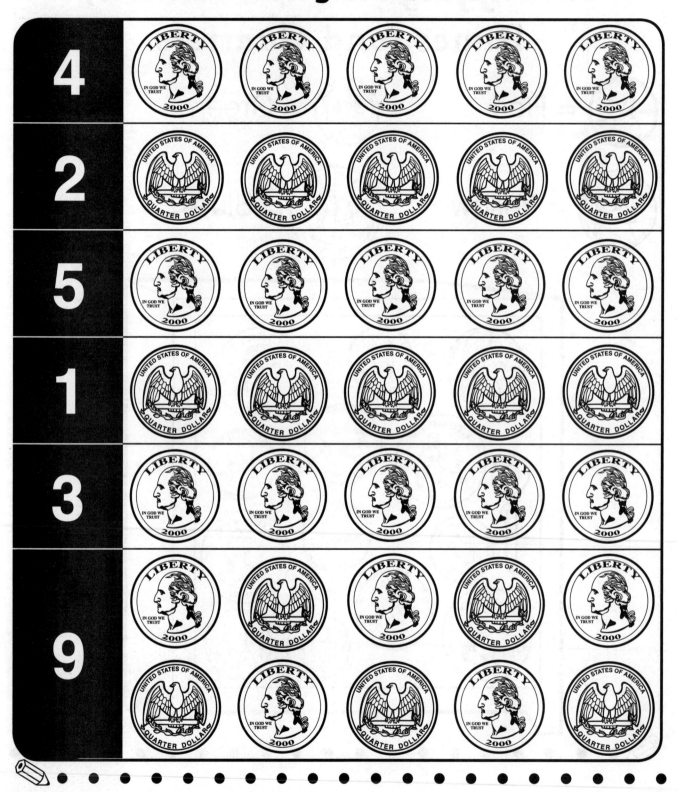

**Directions:** Look at the number before each row of quarters. Color that number of quarters.

# Buying with Quarters

A quarter is worth 25 cents.

1 quarter = 25¢

Count by 25's:

25           50           75          100

Every four quarters = one dollar = $1.00

**Directions:** Look at the price tag on each item. Color the number of quarters needed to buy the item.

Name_____

# Buying with Pennies, Nickels, Dimes, and Quarters

**Directions:** Look at the price tag on each item. Color the number of pennies, nickels, dimes, and quarters needed to buy the item.

# Tallying with Quarters

Shake a quarter in your hands.  Open your hands and drop the quarter on the table.  If the quarter lands on the front side, or *heads* side, make a tally mark in the *heads* row.  If the quarter lands on the back side, or *tails* side, make a tally mark in the *tails* row.  Continue the game until you have reached 10 tally marks on either the *heads* or *tails* side.

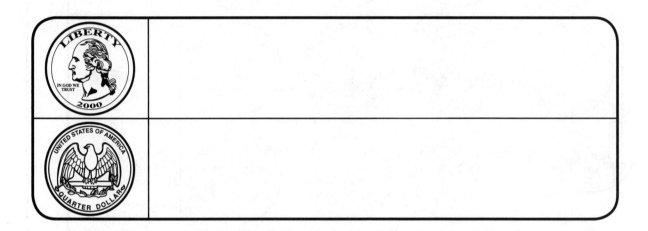

Shake a quarter in your hands.  Open your hands and drop the quarter on the table.  If the quarter lands on the front side, or *heads* side, color in the heads quarter in the column.  If the quarter lands on the back side, or *tails* side, color in the tails quarter.  Do this five times.

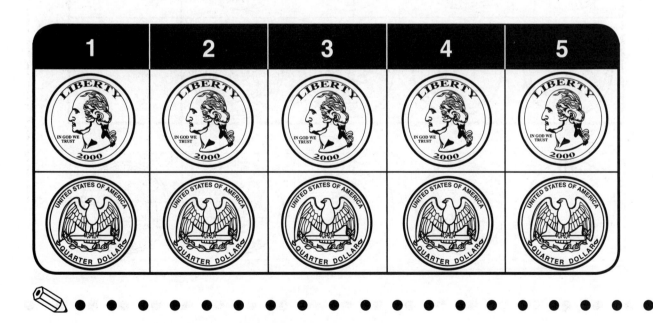

**Directions:** Follow the directions above to use each type of tally table.

# Patterning with Quarters

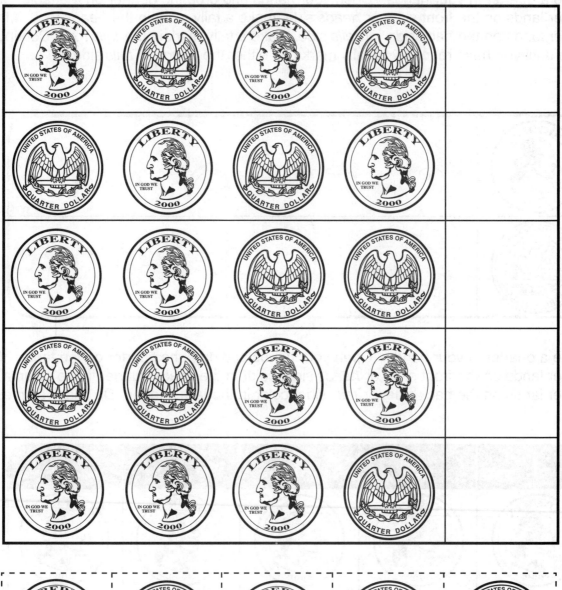

 ● ● ● ● ● ● ● ● ● ● ● ● ● ● ● ● ● ● ●

**Directions:** Look at the row of quarters. Determine whether the next quarter in the pattern will be *heads* or *tails*. Cut out the correct quarters and paste them in the appropriate boxes.

# Patterning with Pennies, Nickels, Dimes, and Quarters

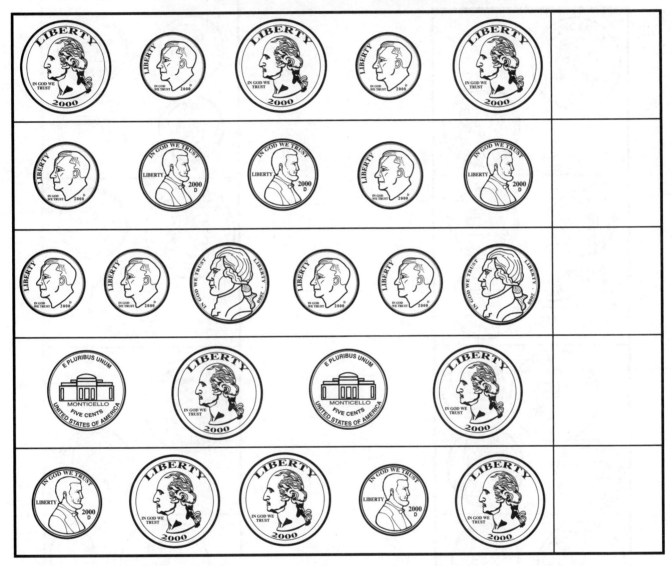

**Directions:** Look at the row of quarters, pennies, nickels, and dimes. Determine whether the next coin in the pattern will be a penny, nickel, dime, or quarter. Cut out the correct coins and paste them in the appropriate boxes.

Name _____

# Matching Sets of Pennies, Nickels, Dimes, and Quarters

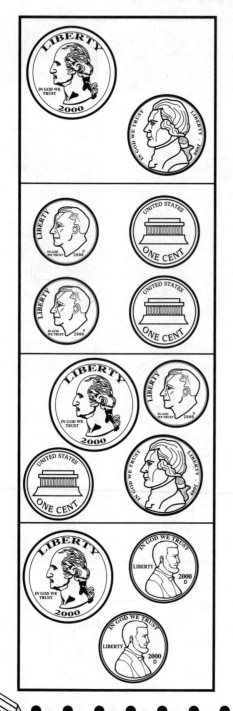

●●●●●●●●●●●●●●●●●●●●●●●●●●●●●

**Directions:** Look at the first box of pennies, nickels, dimes, and quarters on the *left*. Find a box of pennies, nickels, dimes, and quarters on the *right* that contains the same amount. Draw a line to match the sets. Repeat with each of the other boxes of coins.

Name_____

# Graphing Quarters

| Heads or Tails | |
|:---:|:---:|
| 5 | |
| 4 | |
| 3 | |
| 2 | |
| 1 | |

**Quarters**

• • • • • • • • • • • • • • • • • • • •

**Directions:** Count the quarters that show *heads*. Color that number of squares on the graph. Count the quarters that show *tails*. Color that number of squares on the graph.

Name _____

# Graphing Pennies, Nickels, Dimes, and Quarters

| Pennies, Nickels, Dimes, and Quarters | | | | Coins |
|---|---|---|---|---|
| 4 | | | | |
| 3 | | | | |
| 2 | | | | |
| 1 | | | | |

**Directions:** Count the pennies. Color that number of squares on the graph. Count the nickels. Color that number of squares on the graph. Count the dimes. Color that number of squares on the graph. Count the quarters. Color that number of squares on the graph.